Copyright © 2013 by Johnette Napolitano
ISBN 978-1-950565-01-6
All rights reserved. No part of this book may be used or reproduced in any manner whatsoever without written permission except in the case of brief quotations embodied in critical articles and reviews. For information address Crossroad Press at 141 Brayden Dr., Hertford, NC 27944
www.crossroadpress.com

Crossroad Press trade edition

johnette napolitano

rough mix

lyrics & writings, memories & dreams in scratchy black and white as remembered through my gray.

p.o. box 1053
joshua tree ca
92252

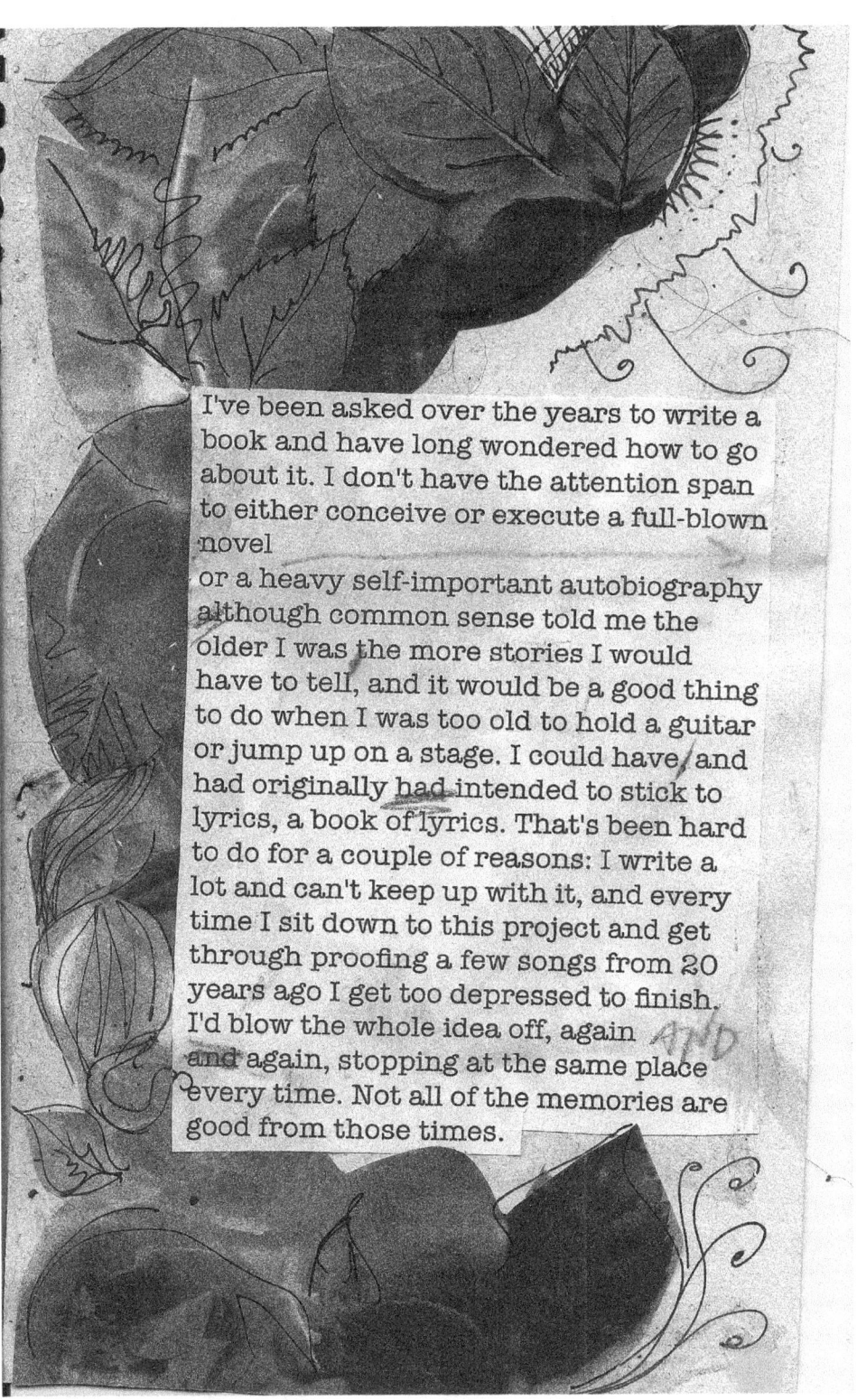

I've been asked over the years to write a book and have long wondered how to go about it. I don't have the attention span to either conceive or execute a full-blown novel

or a heavy self-important autobiography although common sense told me the older I was the more stories I would have to tell, and it would be a good thing to do when I was too old to hold a guitar or jump up on a stage. I could have, and had originally had intended to stick to lyrics, a book of lyrics. That's been hard to do for a couple of reasons: I write a lot and can't keep up with it, and every time I sit down to this project and get through proofing a few songs from 20 years ago I get too depressed to finish. I'd blow the whole idea off, again AND and again, stopping at the same place every time. Not all of the memories are good from those times.

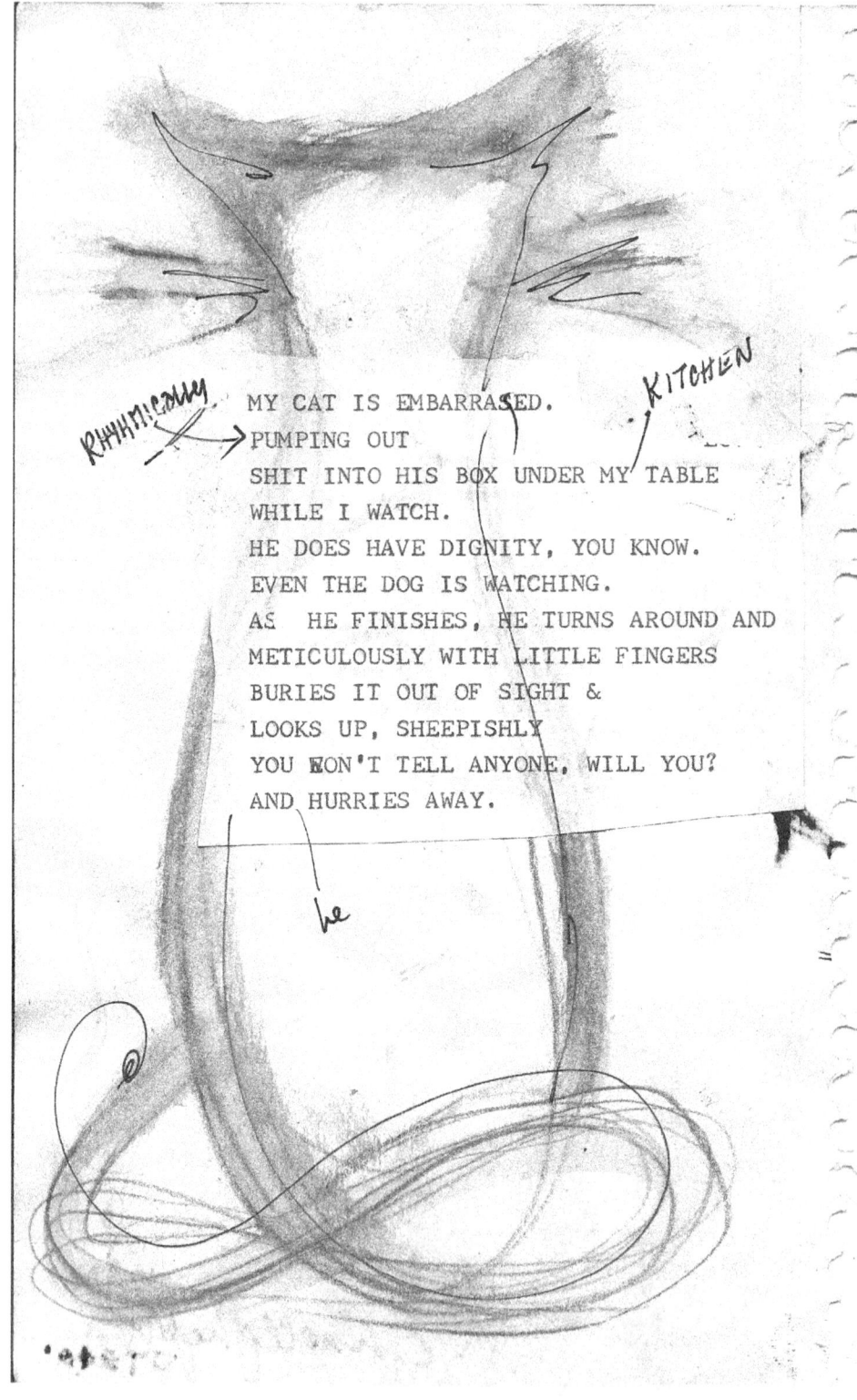

MY CAT IS EMBARRASED.
PUMPING OUT [RHHHYTHMICALLY]
SHIT INTO HIS BOX UNDER MY TABLE [KITCHEN]
WHILE I WATCH.
HE DOES HAVE DIGNITY, YOU KNOW.
EVEN THE DOG IS WATCHING.
AS HE FINISHES, HE TURNS AROUND AND
METICULOUSLY WITH LITTLE FINGERS
BURIES IT OUT OF SIGHT &
LOOKS UP, SHEEPISHLY
YOU WON'T TELL ANYONE, WILL YOU?
AND HURRIES AWAY.

Then something happened in the middle of this whole thing: my Dad got cancer. He has since passed away and it's as if a sun has gone down and shadows will forever be cast from a different angle. So I revisit this whole endeavor through re-shaped eyes and heart and now, indeed, I am all the way back to the beginning.

I've always maintained song lyrics are not poetry, or certainly don't have to be, and formal poetry not meant to be song. At least since the invention of the written word. Great rock and roll does not demand literary genius. "Tutti Frutti" may not be poetry to everyone, but it's definitely rock and roll.

I've tried to choose lyrics that I can still stand to read after all these years and some things that aren't published or recorded yet.

When we made the first record I was working a day job,

and took the Santa Monica Boulevard bus all the way into Century City at 7:00 a.m. in the morning. Every morning

I'd get into my steel-toed French army boots and grab my notebooks

and hike the 4 or so blocks to the bus stop, past the Jewish cemetary by the TV studios, up to Santa Monica. I'd write a lot in my head on those mornings, and on the mornings when the bus, packed to the gills with morning commuters, would blow right by me

and I was screwed and resigned to wait for the next one I'd scribble away, leaned against the cinderblock wall of the carwash behind me. I wanted to,

and I knew I would, see more of the world I'd always known was out there. I was on the streets all the time, since I was a kid, and the people on the street fascinated me. Everybody had a story. Everybody was a character in a crazy scene

Always verging on or often completely spinning wildly out of control.

11/13/08

Bianco's Apt.
Santa Monica & Vine

....I'm subletting my friend Jim Bianco's 3rd floor walkup (I ain't gettin' in that elevator) above the surplus store at Santa Monica & Vine, right across the street from where Gold Star used to be. There's a mini-mall there now, and on this side of the Boulevard is Paramount studios, where we recorded the Pretty & Twisted album, and down a bit on this side there is now a little theatre where there was once a record pressing plant.

In between was a place called G&M Record labels, run by Max and his wife, a sweet German couple. We'd send out the lacquer masters from the studio, huge slabs of smelly plastic, carefully and freshly packed in between blocks of styrofoam and duct taped together like a time-sensitive musical hamburger. You have to get the slabs into the 'bath' soon, or the lacquer deteriorates, so it was a very big deal to maintain temperature and timely delivery to the plant, who sent their runner to Gold Star every day around 4:00.

STILL IN HOLLYWOOD
(Concrete Blonde, Concrete Blonde)

I was walking down the street early this morning
Past the graveyard, voices singin' to me.
I was walking down the street, early this morning
And the silver drops of rain hung from the leaves
And I swear I heard the voices singing to me...
Singing to the rhythm of the beat of my feet,
I swear I heard the voices singing to me -
Keep on, keep on, keep on.

Still in Hollywood!
Oh WOW! Thought I'd be out of here by now.
Still in Hollywood!
My, my I'm running on a wheel and I don't know why
I don't know why.

And on the bus today, I met the queen of L.A. -
At least she said she was and who am I to say?
She was sixty-five and full of life,
She had purple-painted cheeks
And glitter on her eyes
And the troll on the corner, I flipped him a quarter
And he looked at me and smiled.
He wasn't abused, he wasn't confused,
He had nothing to gain and less to lose

Still in Hollywood,
Oh WOW! Thought I'd be out of here by now.
Still in Hollywood!
My, my I'm running like a rat and I don't know why

And so it's three A.M., I'm out walking again.
I'm just a spot on the sidewalk in the city of sin.
He doesn't give a fuck, he's living under a truck.
You know it coulda been me, guess it's just my luck.
But I swear I hear the voices singing to me -
Keep on, keep on, keep on.

Still in Hollywood...

So, ideally, within the time window the lacquers would be bathed and set and the positives (lacquer masters) would be made into negatives (metal pressing plates) that would press up the vinyl records (positives again) and the labels (Max) would be done at the same time. Dave Gold, possibly the greatest pioneer/innovator in the history of Los Angeles recorded audio would spend hours drawing for me on scraps of paper where the bass frequency laid in the groove of a vinyl record. How the needle laid against the sides of the little 'canyons' that were the grooves of the disc and read the sounds, how it was only possible to squeeze a certain amount of those sounds in the little canyons of grooves. How the louder things needed to be and the more music people were wanting on vinyl, there just wasn't the space. Too many songs, too much time, and the grooves have to be narrower and crowded together and level suffers. Too much bass and the needle simply jumps right up out of the groove, literally kicked up and out - disc mastering is a serious art, and Dave was the best. We're talking vinyl records, oldschool. This was 1980 and it was oldschool even then, but the punks and new indie labels were making 45's and real records. The biggest customer of the pressing plant was a Mexican guy who owned a label called Fiesta, and would bring wads and wads of cash up from Mexico. When money ran low at the plant, every damn thing made of vinyl got thrown into the hopper: old shower curtains, anything. Click, pop, click, pop. They make plug-ins to get sounds in the studio like that now, but it was really just crappy vinyl

"Anyway I jumped at the chance to spend a couple of weeks here at Bianco's, who is a great musician and a true road dog. I needed a little push...it's a properly seedy old Hollywood apartment building, like all the old Hollywood apartments I'd ever lived in. Old banisters on the stairs under 15 coats of paint, an old-fashioned icebox in the kitchen now used as cupboard space, a nice clawfoot bathtub without the feet, all kinds of little Murphy-style dropdown seats and shelves, and I guess that little sliding door next to the toilet with a massive black hole of a space that drops down 3 stories was a dumbwaiter? Or laundry chute, maybe....in any case, I'm feelin' it, and as Jimmy and I bump his overpacked suitcase down the stairs and he hauls off to the airport there are two pigeons that have come in from the window ledge on the landing of the 3rd floor, pecking and kissing in the hallway. "They're making out!", Jimmy says, heaving his half of the suitcase down the stairs, and I'm careful to not trip over my feet as I follow him down with my half.

"...and if you're lucky," he continues, backing down, almost to the ground floor now, "the whole place smells like excellent Mexican food on some nights."

"So how haunted is this place?" I have to ask, immediately. No way it's not, I'm thinking to myself, struggling to keep my balance as I ease myself down the stairs one at a time.

"It did burn down once." Jim says, which is enough for me, and we load him into his car at the curb before the meter ran out.

So I guess I'm back at the scene of the crime, as it were. Things are different but it feels the same. But I'm not the same. But maybe I want to be. You can lose yourself in the city, nobody's paying attention. I wonder if I drop dead who will find me, so I take the time to copy my info onto a jump drive I attach to a keyring alongside Jim's front door key.

What a strange thing to be back here..on this corner, of all places. I'm in a strange state of mind. It's a full moon. Grabbed some Thai from across the street, a dusty bottle of Pinot Noir from the little market.

It's just like my old place. Places, even. Because these old Hollywood apartments had massive closets (a lot of them housed the contract players from the studios in the old days) Jim's turned his massive closet into a cozy sleeping pod/ library with a little lamp, a nice thick comforter ('high thread count!' he says, proudly) and it's dark and soft and I'm thumbing through books and before I drift off I remind myself to wash everything before he comes home in the laundry room across the hall. I'm doing the right thing. I need to get all the way back to the beginning.

RUN RUN RUN
(Concrete Blonde/Walking In London)

you get crazy
you get tossed
you go running around
like you know you're gonna fall off
he knows what you need
he knows how much you want
knock familiar
welcome in
can't believe that you let him
introduce you as a friend
but you're always polite
in case you need him again
not again
can't believe the way I see you
run, run, run.
can't believe the way you bleed when you
run, run, run.
are you having fun?

your hands are shaking
lips are cracked
you swore
I heard you swear
you were never going back
only one more time
just this one more night
and so again
you lose the fight
can't believe the way you need to
run, run, run
can't believe the way I see you
run, run, run
are we having fun?
run, run, run.

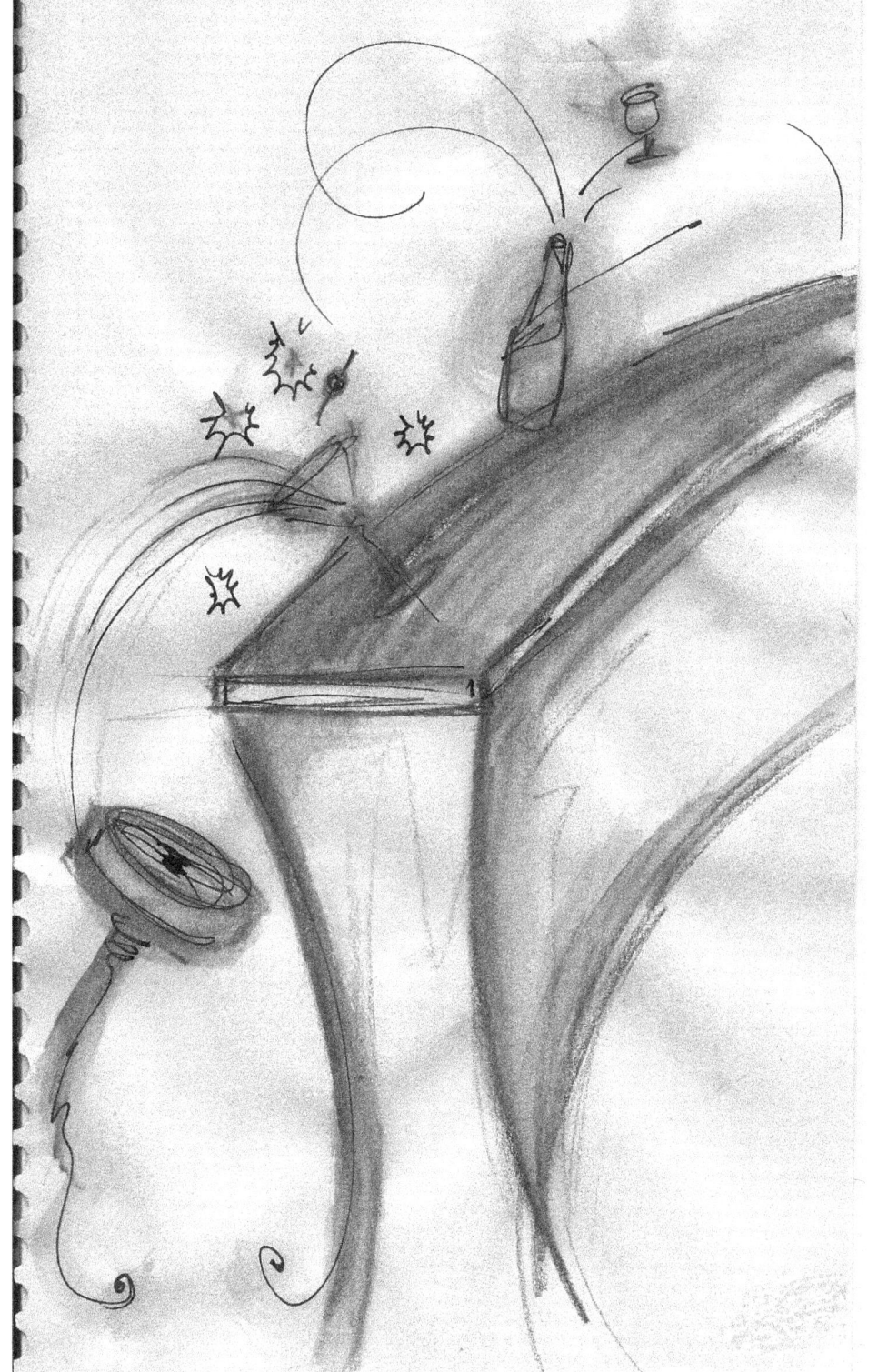

Back in the day there was a guy on the punk scene I'll call Sam who was the local speed dealer down off Santa Monica Boulevard in an old apartment building across the street from the Formosa Cafe. Speed was the drug of choice then for us street rats, and I have to say, we were a scruffy lot but we were always making things happen, starting labels and booking crazy gigs and hanging out at Kinko's all night making flyers and fanzines. Everybody in those days was on the hustle. Cocaine was for the record company pigs but we had our $10 bags of crank and drank a lot of booze and played a whole lot of songs very, very fast.

Anyway one day I popped over after work to Sam's apartment. Sam was a tall, skinny guy with thin, greasy dirty blonde hair and thick coke-bottle glasses that always made him look a little loony, but when he was buggin' on speed it was truly bizarre, his big giant rolling bug eyes behind his thick glasses. I knocked at the thin, cheap apartment door. I could hear the TV on. No answer. I knocked again, a little louder this time.

Nothing.

I knocked again, this time louder, because of course I want my damn speed and when somebody on speed wants their speed it can get pretty tense, but you know how it is, you can't be bitchy with your drug dealer because of course you know damn well you will need him in the future a whole lot more than he will ever need you.

"Come in." I hear a small voice from inside, pretty stupid considering he's a drug dealer, I thought, and slowly cracked open the door. It was pitch black inside the little cramped apartment except for the little flickering light of the TV screen in the corner. Sam was sitting there next to the TV in a chair patiently and meticulously unravelling a rope, the yellow plastic woven kind, like a water-ski rope. The unravelled part of the rope stretched clean across the room and I wondered how many days he'd been doing this, sitting in the dark, unravelling a plastic rope. Why he was doing it I knew better than to even contemplate, he was truly in a state and I just wanted to get my little square white paper envelope of speed and get the hell out of there. I didn't even ask Sam what he was doing; and he offered no explanation. I popped the Foster's I'd brought with me for something to do during the minimum time I would need to spend there chatting with Sam during the transaction and offered Sam some, even though the whole apartment was piled everywhere a foot deep with beer bottles.

HOLLYWOOD & VINE
(Johnette Napolitano/unreleased)

Honey,
you got a light?
it's finally Friday night
I've had a shot or two o' Jack
& I gotta say that I feel allright

Sorry, I gotta go
I'm in a hurry, don't you know
she's a piece...
she's an angel,
takes me up when I'm feeling low

Man,
 you gotta see her,
  she's so fine..

I got a date tonight
under the street light
at Hollywood and Vine.

He takes me to Musso & Frank
He's got money in the bank
He keeps me in martinis
and plenty of gasoline in my tank

she'll be waiting for me there
shiny dress and shiny hair
I don't know how she pays her rent,
I don't know and I don't care

brother, I gotta say
she's so damn fine..

I got a date tonight
under the streetlight
at Hollywood and Vine.

Sam got up to find the speed, looking through drawers, scratching his chin, remembering, walking in tiny circles in the tiny kitchen as I sat quietly drinking my beer thinking this just sucks in general and I'm not diggin' this scene at all. I feel like I'm starting to itch. Sam, *how*

working up a head of steam and growing more and more frustrated, starts banging things around and stomping back and forth in between the tiny kitchen and the bathroom and ripping into jacket pockets and turning over plates. He even lifted up the TV to look under it. I was getting nervous, as I'd already given him my $60 and would have a hell of a hard time asking for it back. He was starting to really lose it now, clutching and pulling at his hair. "FUCK! Where the FUCK! GOD! DAMMIT! Where the FUCK IS IT?" And he's just going off like he's having a seizure, he's so angry, standing there stamping his feet amongst all that yellow plastic unravelled rope. I have no idea how long this went on but it certainly seemed like a hell of a long time and I remember pretending I was still drinking my beer when in fact I had been finished for awhile. I was too

scared to try to leave, then finally Sam found the speed, which had been in his shirt pocket the whole time. Shaking and pretty disgusted with the whole creepy scene and with myself, I let myself out into the hot, greasy Hollywood summer air and never saw him again.

TRUE
(Concrete Blonde- lyrics Napolitano)

well when I've had enough
I'll get a pickup truck
and I'll drive away
I'll take my last 10 bucks
just as far as it will go
well sometimes I'm easily fooled
I take a painful step
and I get knocked back 2
I do all I can
and it's all I can do
but I'm True.
and if I had a choice
I'd take the voice I've got
'cause it was hard to find
you know I've come too far
to wind up right back where I started
they tell me who I should be
I'll never let those monkeys
make a mess of me
I do all I can and it's all I can do
but I'm True.

one more sunset
lay my head down
True.
one more sunrise
open my eyes up
True.

They talk you up
and then then they talk you down
and you begin to doubt
sometimes the reasons seem to very far away
but I'll stop breathing today
if I can't walk proud I'd rather walk away
I do all I can and it's all I can do
but I'm True.
I give all I have
and I give it to you,
True.

Early days, early days. This was on a cassette of instrumental music Jim Mankey had given me to listen to. He'd had something else on the tape that he wanted me to like but I flipped out over this piece of music. I loved it so much that we put the instrumental on the first Concrete Blonde record as well as the vocal version. When I look back on everything it took to get to this place, right now, it amazes me. I can't say I didn't always know what I wanted to do, but had no idea what it would take, which was simply everything. I'd been singing and playing and writing since I was a kid, working since I was 15 and staying up all night in the bathroom with cassette players learning how to bounce harmonies back and forth, writing on the bus on the way to work. Hitting up every club in Hollywood for a gig, then if we got one half the time we weren't playing for anybody but the bartender. Years of shitty jobs and hauling your amps up flights of stairs and not even making gas money.

After years of this you may finally get some attention and they will then tell you you're doing it all wrong. Among other things I heard from people who turned out to be massive in, or what was once, the music business, was that I couldn't write and Jim Mankey couldn't play guitar. I didn't realize raw talent was nothing more than someone else's blank canvas for someone's elses vision. We didn't fit the template in any way. I'd taken up the bass in sheer desperation as we couldn't keep a bass player. No one wanted to be in the band at all. We had no following, no deal, no money. "Shouldn't there be 4 people in the band?" the suits would ask. I pointed out I was doing the job of 2 people, playing bass and singing lead.

I have met several 'artists' who desperately need someone to point them in the direction of the toilet let alone know who the hell they were who or what they were about at all. The music business is chock-full of frustrated artists who either didn't have the ability or the balls to stick it out for art's sake so the next best thing was to park themselves behind desks to be near it all and unfortunately have checkbooks and some of them - not all, but some - really, really fucking hated you for doing what it is they themselves had originally wanted to do but didn't.

All I knew was that this shit sounded pretty good to me, our friends, and our families. A less-and-less naive, ignorant, spunky, bus-riding, white-trash, tequila-drinking combat-boot wearing crazy little chick told the overpaid sadistic upper level VP's they were mistaken, but offer after offer they either wanted to get us to cover some classic rock tune (that was before they called it Classic Rock, I'm pretty sure), or commit to one direction or another and we just couldn't be placed, like some weird unidentifiable mutant-hybrid sea creature caught in a tuna net off the coast of Japan. We were who we were, we weren't being difficult and uncooperative, it just wasn't possible to be anyone else other than who we were.

Concrete Blonde's guitarist, who absolutely hated it. He gave me a whole lot of grief about it, he wanted me to use this other track that was just about as mediocre as it gets, but as any Concrete Blonde fan knows, I was right. This was, and is, a brilliant piece of music.

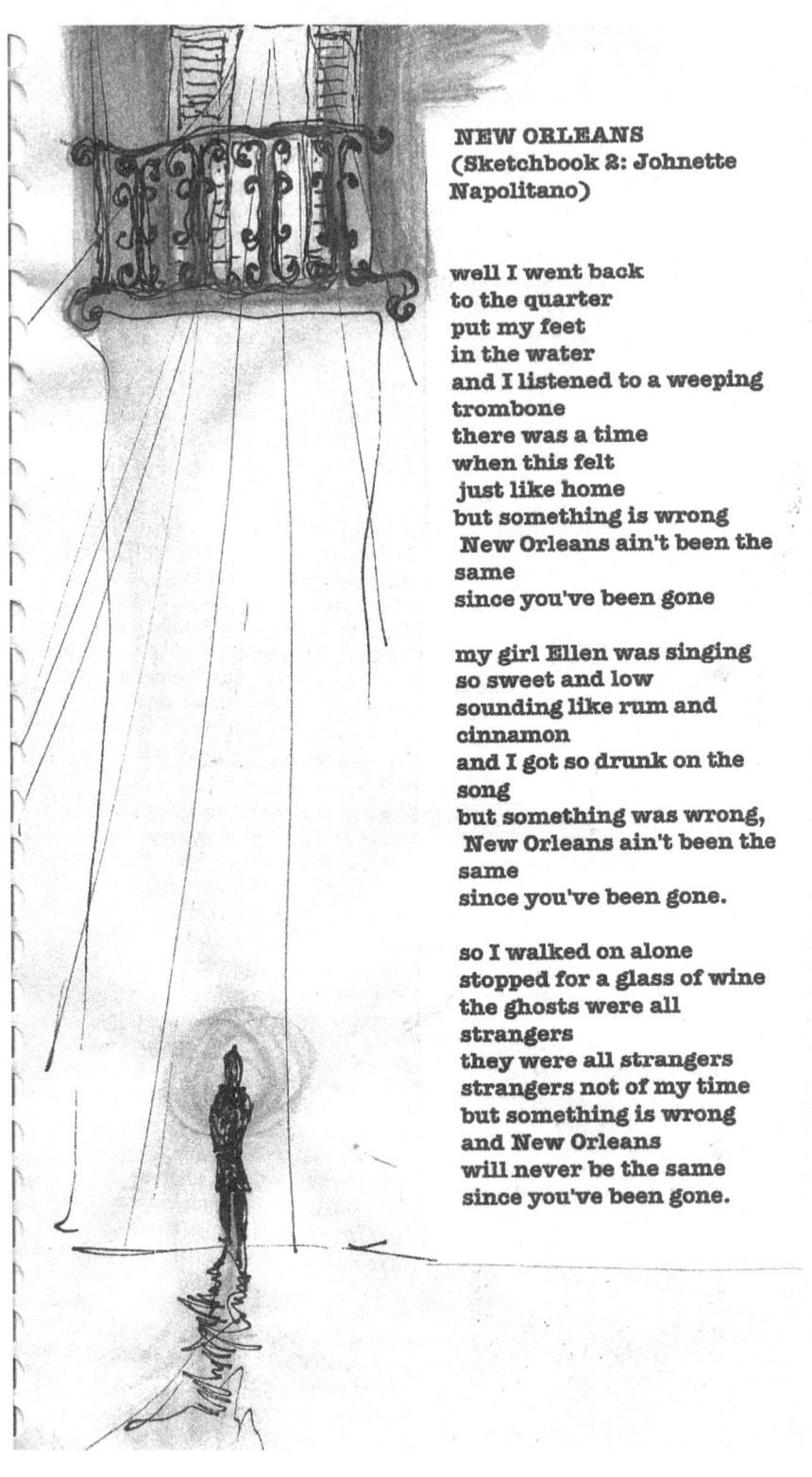

NEW ORLEANS
(Sketchbook 2: Johnette Napolitano)

well I went back
to the quarter
put my feet
in the water
and I listened to a weeping
trombone
there was a time
when this felt
 just like home
but something is wrong
 New Orleans ain't been the same
since you've been gone

my girl Ellen was singing
so sweet and low
sounding like rum and
cinnamon
and I got so drunk on the
song
but something was wrong,
 New Orleans ain't been the same
since you've been gone.

so I walked on alone
stopped for a glass of wine
the ghosts were all
strangers
they were all strangers
strangers not of my time
but something is wrong
and New Orleans
will never be the same
since you've been gone.

Bloodletting (The Vampire Song)

there's a crack in the mirror and a bloodstain on the bed   there's a crack in the mirror and a bloodstain on the bed

o you were a vampire and baby I'm walking dead   you were a vampire and baby I'm walking dead

I've got the ways and means to New Orleans
goin' down by the river where it's warm and green

I'm gonna have a drink and walk around
I've got a lot to think about

there's a rocking chair in the shadow down the hall
I see something there in the shadow down the hall

o you were a vampire and now I'm worth nothing at all   you were a vampire and now I'm worth nothing at all

I've got the ways and means to New Orleans
I'm going down by the river where it's warm and green

I'm gonna have a drink and walk around
I've got a lot to think about..

New Orleans was the first city outside of LA on our first tour we'd ever went out on. I fell in love with the city right away and started spending time off down there. 'Interview With A Vampire' was massive back then. Being Californian, the South was mysterious and foreign to me, the huge silent cypress trees draped in moss, the little gaslamps flickering like fireflies glowing in the French Quarter. Books and bricks and dark old adobe bars where I'd spend hours with my notebook drinking wine. I'd just go down and lose myself in the atmosphere,
feeling like I was being watched all the time. Indeed I was. Unwritten words and music hung in the fog, waiting to be manifested.

One time I was in a little guesthouse in the Garden District, a great little place with filled-in fireplaces and bookshelves filled with old books,
pages green around the edges from the constant damp with titles like "Young Abraham Lincoln". I was reading in bed and nodding off to sleep one night - for

some reason I slept a lot in that room - when, in the dark, eyes closed, I felt someone climb up on the big antique bed with me, one knee first, a right knee on my left side, and then swinging a leg over me and I felt the bed sink on my right side. Someone was straddling me!

I was completely, completely terrified. I hadn't heard anyone come in, as a matter of fact had jammed a chair up under the doorknob of the flimsy old wooden door that led out to the hallway noticing the lock had been broken at least once.

I could hardly breathe. Whoever they were, I felt their knees on either side of me. I didn't know whether to pretend I was asleep or start screaming. I decided, finally, to open my eyes, which I did, and there was no one there. I was in bed alone.

The next morning I asked the man at the desk, "is this place haunted?"

"What room are you in?" he asked, not looking up.

"12"

"Yeah, well some people say there's something going on. Everybody says they get real sleepy in that room."

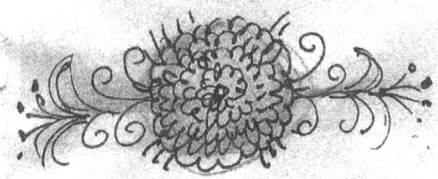

"Oh, there are more walking around down here dead than alive!" DeLoris used to say. I met Miss D almost 30 years ago at the Bottom of The Cup Tearoom where she was a psychic reader. She's well into her 80's now and retired but lived up above the shop and from her wrought-iron balcony you could smell the pralines cooking on the corner and listen to the music and parades and drunks and laughter, even though she'd never touched a drop in her life. "I don't like the smell" she'd say. She'd been around, Miss D., and had even been tried as a 'witch' back in 1962 in Arkansas. She won, but not after a long trial and death threats from the local Holy Rollers. I told her I had to write a script, it had to be a movie. "Wait until I'm gone" she'd said, "I don't want to go through that again. Seeing some my closest friends in that courthouse, pretending not to know me." She was, and is, my teacher, wise

;andmother, and friend. I helped her move out of the upstairs place when she moved to Metairie before Katrina. You haven't lived in until you've moved a woman in her eighties out of a place she'd lived for decades: boxes of letters, clothes, crystals, souvenirs from years in her profession. A tackle box from the bottom of a lake found next to a body she'd helped the police find. She's living with her son now. When I'm in New Orleans I always pass her balcony and look up. Quite a lady, quite a life. New Orleans hasn't quite been the same without her.

and green   I'm gonna have a drink   and walk   around;   I've got a lot to think   about..

where it's warm

I'm going down by the   river

to New Orleans

I've got the ways and   means

Miss deLoris: San Francisco
WWII

SONG FOR KIM
(Concrete Blonde: Johnette Napolitano)

Oh Kim,
your diary said
the voices calling you from
the edge
they finally called you
away
you know I hear them, too.
they're telling me to stay
Oh Kim
remember when
we made a million plans
and we believed in them.
angry words
ring in my head
I'd give every song I gave in
me
to get you back again.
she said I could,
she said hold on, hold out
'cause it's good.
she said
 you're right
she said hold on, hold out
'cause I know that you can
fight
I know that you can
you're right again
there is an easy way
out of this world
I'm staying
I wonder why
it may be all I have

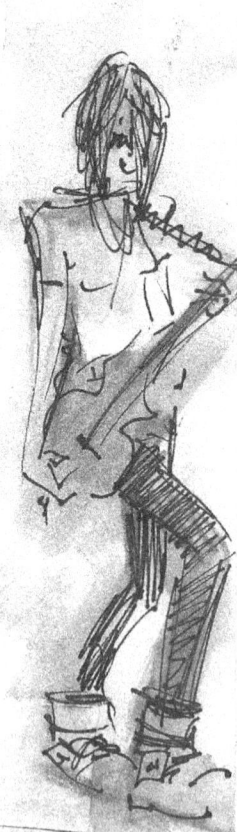

but it's mine,
my time.

Kim was a spunky, streetwise, hardcore punk girl from upstate New York I met in a coffee shop at Santa Monica & Vine when I worked at Gold Star Studios. I ate there on my 1/2 hour lunch every day and would work on lyrics. The place has long since been the Three O'Clubs bar in Hollywood, but Kim was a waitress there and had a very special vibe. She'd been in Hollywood trying to put a band together herself, and was out and about on the punk scene. Kim's story was rough: her stepfather had been some sort of high-ranking Government official and had been molesting her since she was 11 or so. Little Kim told her grandmother, who slapped her face and accused her of provoking her stepfather, details long lost to me now, but stepdad indeed was busted down to Long Beach cop from what I recall. Kim and I became good friends and I wanted to help her with her music. She wrote smart, dark lyrics and crude but catchy bass hooks, and had reams of poems and songs with titles like 'Tax Religion' and 'Lady Killer' about a serial rapist.

She was a lot more worldly than I, my friend Kim, and introduced me to a lot of punk and postpunk; and we hung around Hollywood a lot in those days and I'd try like hell to get something together, some kind of rehearsal, something done, and Kim would show up with whoever she was fucked up with who is who would be the bandmember that day who would be as fucked up as Kim was, and I'd hold down a riff for awhile but after a few of these sessions I lost interest. As much as I loved her and the songs, or at least the potential of the songs, it was all too crazy as everything was at the time in Hollywood. The Gun Club rehearsed in the next room and everybody was just smacked out, just off the planet, and as whacked out as I was at the time the heroin thing was too heavy, too scary for me. To add to it all Kim had gotten herself pregnant and was delighted. She'd started buying baby clothes at thrift stores, thinking of baby names, never naming the father, who could have been any one of several people. She was gorgeous, her white Goth skin and ink black choppy mop of hair, her ripped up old men's suit jackets and army boots and safety pins and big, pregnant belly, walking around Hollywood, smoking, drinking, just being Kim.

She had the baby prematurely which was no surprise, but the baby was born blue, that is dead, and after 15 minutes was revived but left partially paralyzed on one side, brain damage unknown, future developmental problems unknown. A lot would depend on Kim's attention as a mother, and she was a sweet mother, working Michelle's little limbs, taking her to get her special little boots. The little girl was a tiny, perfect replica of her free-spirited, tragic mom, black hair and black little eyes, one lazy and crossed inward toward her little nose.

From what I remember now it was 1982 and Kim and the baby had been living with a nice young guy for awhile, and she was riding in the truck with him on Olympic Blvd. in L.A., a fast moving artery through the city, and she just opened the passenger side door and rolled out onto the street into traffic. Michelle had been in her little carrier on the seat beside her. I forgot how I found out. I remember finding the apartment on Franklin she'd just moved into and was so proud of, an airy, light upper floor. I remember identifying her apartment contents for the landlady. She hadn't even unpacked everything.

She just didn't know how hard it would be.

I remember her real father, long estranged from her mother, calling, and I remember not really knowing what to say. I wound up with her diaries and crazy 1920's monkeyfur coat and armadillo purse and records and old Rolling Stones and Free Press papers she'd found in the basement of the Malaga Castle, where a lot of the punks lived and had been the notorious basement offices of the Los Angeles Free Press, finally surrounded and busted by the cops. Everything had been piled out onto the street, and Kim had trunks full of all kinds of 70's revolutionary activist archives.

That was the first time I'd lost someone really close to me, and it shocked me. I thought of her often over the years, she truly loved rock and roll, it was much more important to her than it was to me. She was so romantic about it.

She was the real deal and I miss her. As far as I know, she never did name Michelle's real father. Michelle was hers, something, someone of hers alone, the only family she had and she really loved her baby. I guess, I don't know, it all added up to be too much one day.

When I Was A Fool
(Concrete Blonde: Group Therapy)

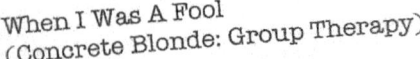

I re-read silly lines
that made sense at the time
pages all stained with tears and red wine
and I walk through the airport,
read magazines
every face that I see
so much younger than me
and I smile to myself,
'cause I don't even miss
my glorious past or the lips that I've kissed
and I think to myself,
how easy this is..
easy to breathe
 easy to live

and I wonder why I tear myself in two?
over how to be, what to say and what to do
I know you liked me better then
I know you liked me better when

I was a fool.

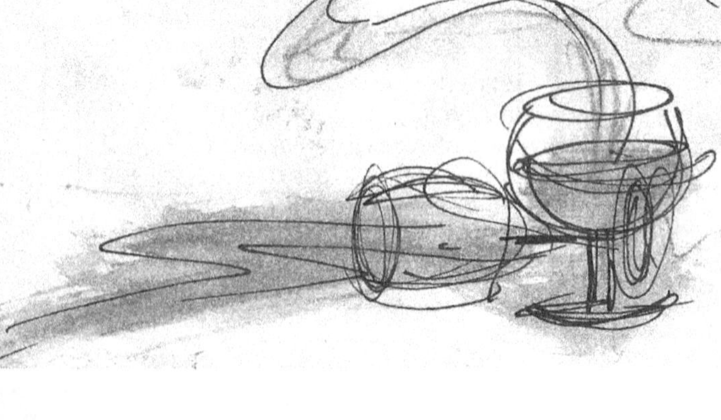

so I live in these days
but I still have some old ways
'cause the future,
somehow,
has yet to arrive
and I see all around me the women on time
kids & divorces & crisis in midlife
so do I surrender and give up a dream
for a brick in the wall and a washing machine
grow up and get real
for a kid in his teens
who won't care what I've done
where I've been
what I've seen

and I wonder why I tear myself in two?
over who to be, what to say and what to do
and I know you liked me better then
and I know you liked me better when

                                        I was a fool.

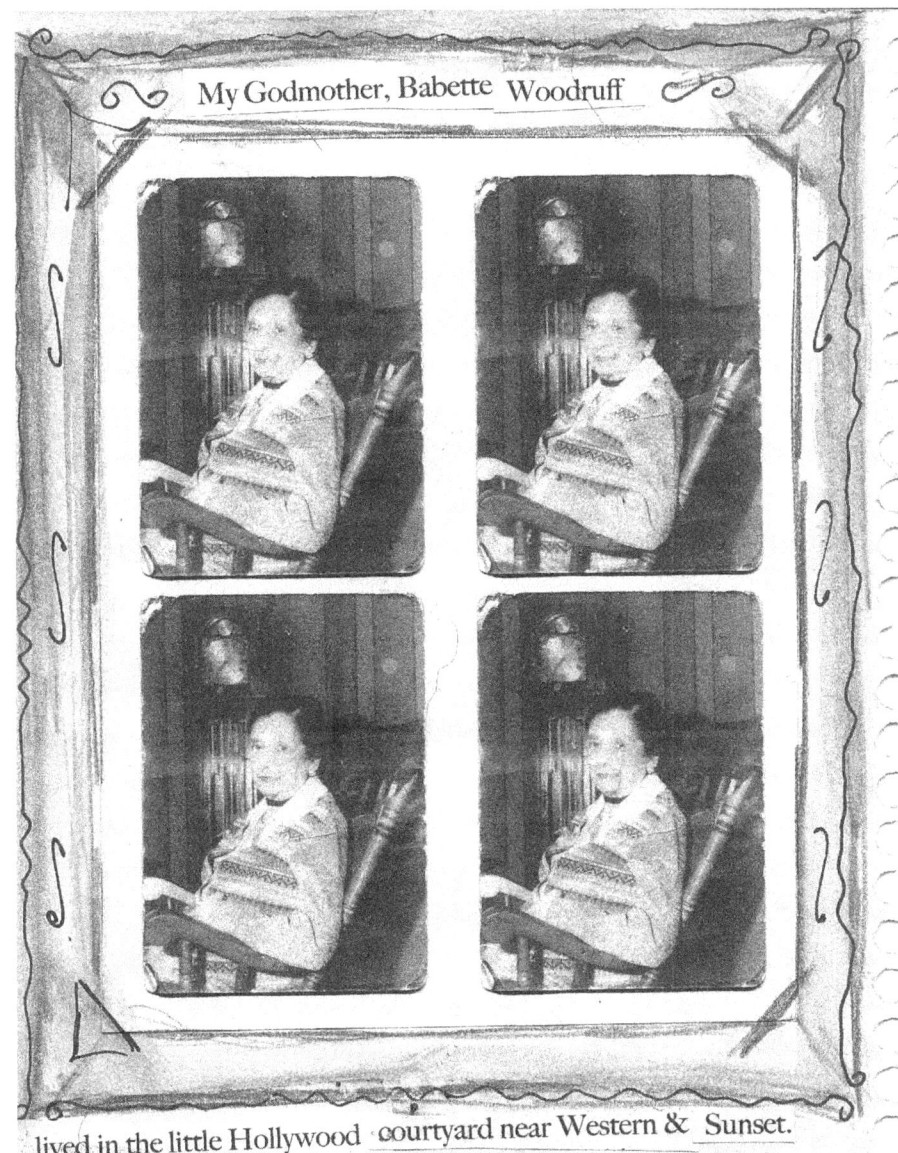

My Godmother, Babette Woodruff

..lived in the little Hollywood courtyard near Western & Sunset. Other notable residents included my Grandmother and Bela Lugosi. She was amazing, grew and fried green tomatoes and had a writing desk that belonged to Abraham Lincoln. There was a long crack in the fireplace where lightning had come down and struck her recliner right after she'd gotten up to go to the kitchen. "You must go to Europe" she would say. She had long black hair and was beautifully mysterious.

I see the ghosts beside you

laughing in the ether

they're playing cards around you

as you sip your coffee

I see the ghosts behind you

leaning over shoulders

amused at your wasting words on

little conversations

I hear the ghosts above you

singing through my head

I see you try to silence them

and quiet them instead

but the ghosts are
always with you

you must know they'll
always be

I know the ghost

I know the ghost

because the ghost is me

I was very small when I told her I wanted to be an artist. "A commercial artist" she'd said. I didn't know what that meant, I wanted to be Vincent Van Gogh and live in an artists' cottage and paint in a beret all day. She and her husband, Christopher Columbus Woodruff, are in

the Hollywood Forever

Cemetary together.

days and dAys

The dirty leaves are sailing
on a hot wind ocean
the summer comes
& summer goes
& always has & will
& something somewhere
that you said
goes ricochet
all through my head
& flashing like a neon sign
the time stand still

Hours of forever
Coming all together
at the crossroads of a
minute
& you and me were in it
& I never saw it coming,
never saw it fade away
Today, today, today....
days and days
days and days

& still the whining of the
wheels
sounds closest to the way I
feel &
winter comes & winter goes,
& always has & will
Another hour, another day,
another year
you pissed away
Remember walking in the
rain?

I'm walking there still.

Like every heart to beat before
& every wave to kiss a shore
I'm not the first, I'm not the last...
& soon to be your past
But every mourning, when the light
comes creeping in around my eyes
another future falls behind
the one I had I mind

Hours of forever
Coming all together
at the crossroads of a minute.
& you and me were in it
& I never saw it coming,
never saw it fade away
Today, today, today....

days and days
days and days

DATE THUR FEB 3RD
BEFORE SHOW
OVERNIGHT
493 MILES FROM OMAHA

CITY MINNEAPOLIS
AFTER SHOW
OVERNIGHT TO CHICAGO
411 MILES

CITY CHICAGO
AFTER SHOW
AT HOTEL

DATE SUN FEB 6TH
BEFORE SHOW
DRIVE FROM CHICAGO
TO DETROIT
279 MILES

CITY DETROIT
AFTER SHOW
OVERNIGHT TO TORONTO
236 MILES

BREAKFAST
RESTAURANT   YES
ROOM SERVICE   12PM-11:30PM
HEALTH CLUB   12PM-11PM
CHECK-IN TIME YES
CHECK-OUT TIME 4AM
               11AM-9TH FEB

TIMES

LOAD IN   1PM
S/C CB   4PM
S/C SB   5PM
DINNER   BUYOUT
DOORS   7PM
SB   8-8:45PM
CB   9:15PM
CURFEW   11PM

The road then, it wasn't like it is now. That was pre-cellphone, pre-laptop, it was better in a lot of ways but of course I can't see now how we ever got along without these things. I wouldn't know where to start with a road story, there are too many. There's the time my tampon fell out onstage. There's the time I had to put my cat in the fridge in the RV driving through the desert in 116 degree heat to make the gig in Chicago after 2 flat tires and getting there right after the opening act came offstage, only to shoot a couple of nervous tequilas and pass out after the first song. The time the three of us were on the way to the gig in the back of a

cab, scared to death as the cab driver, in a fit of road rage, informed us he has a gun under the seat. Ah, and then the time, when we were on Sting's tour, and it was a long tour and we used to drive right after the shows at night..

. the label had a party for us in Kansas City and for once, I wanted to party after the show   I had an asshole for a tour manager who said if I wasn't back at the hotel on the bus by 7:30 a.m. they would leave without me. I woke up across town in the morning and missed the bus by 15 minutes, the prick had left without me. Now that I think of, it, why the hell didn't my BAND wait for me? Pussies. Anyway, Indeed I had to, in my streaked face and stage clothes and sweat from the night before get myself to the airport and on a plane that they weren't certain I should have been allowed on to get myself to the next city, land, and get to the ultradome in time to go onstage the next night. I fired that guy before the last show and we had the best time on the bus we'd had the whole tour, that Napoleonic bastard. Still, my band were pussies.

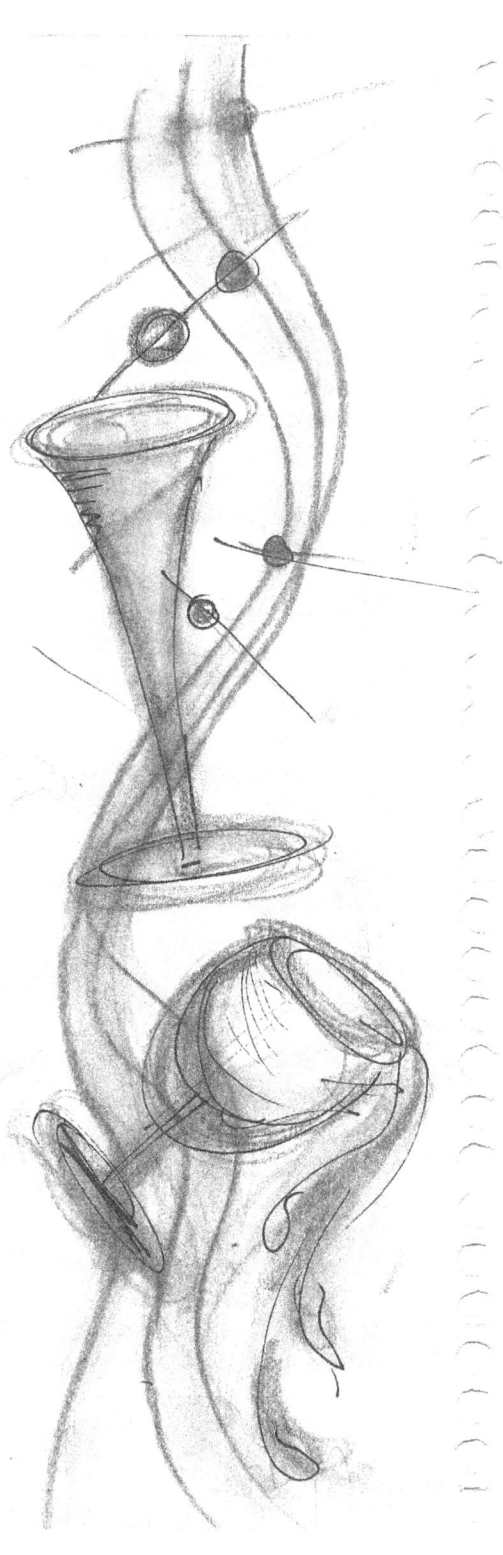

You have to stay awake in the city. You have to watch your back, you have to listen, pay attention. L.A. has always had her share of gang warfare, and that's really what this song was about, the innocent bystanders, the bullets coming through the walls, hitting babies, innocent kids. I heard on the radio recently a story about a woman in church whose baby started crying and wouldn't stop. She took the baby to the restroom to change her diaper and found a bullet in it that had apparently been fired up in the air and come down through the ceiling, miraculously lodging in the baby's diaper. This was about how one split second in time can change the course of many lives, many destinies. This was about someone leaving to go to school that day never knowing they'd never be coming home that night. This was about the bad cops, the ones abusing their positions.

Years ago I had a neighbor who was a Viet Nam vet. Seemed a nice enough guy, would come over every once in awhile to see if I had any wine or weed. He was certainly paranoid, but when I think of it now, and this was 30 years ago, it makes me wonder. He'd had a dummy sitting in a chair at the kitchen table by the window, dressed like him.

Every evening he would take out his gun and shoot it down into his front lawn, just so people knew he had it. He swore one day all 'they' would have to do would be to shut down all the gas stations in LA and paralyze the city, because 'they' controlled them. I was living alone, waitressing, playing guitar and very young. One night I was over at his place and we were smoking and hanging out, and he took the gun out from under the cushion of his overstuffed easy chair, and started waving it around..clicking the hammer, smiling maniacally. I was starting to get nervous.

He very slowly raised the barrel

of the gun to my left temple, and I closed my eyes, I couldn't move. I couldn't breathe. I was absolutely frozen. I felt the cold barrel of the gun on the left side of my face as he started to slowly stroke my cheek with it, outlining my jaw, my hairline. I then felt his lips on the right side of my face, kissing my right cheek every so softly, my temple, my eyelid. The cold steel on the left, the warm lips on the right. My closed eyelids couldn't contain the hot tears that started to roll down my face, rivers, dripping down my chin. 'Please don't'. I whispered, utterly terrified. In my mind I could tomorrow's paper with the story in it, Viet Nam vet rapes and kills local girl, and I was totally convinced I was going to die. I don't know how long it went on but of course it seemed like an eternity. Then he stopped. I heard the gun click, and opened my eyes. He stood there with a strange expression on his face, and I wonder what it was. The his arms were hanging at his sides, gun uncocked. The

[AROUND THE CORNER]

moment had passed. I tore out of the house, and back home where I called the police. They came, heard my story, went over to his house, and asked if he owned a gun. 'Yes' he'd said. 'Can we see it?' they'd said, and he pulled it out from under the cushion, where I'd told them it would be. 'Have you had it out this evening?' they'd asked, and he'd said no.

They left, nothing they could do. I'd told my landlady about the whole thing and she didn't believe me, he'd seemed so nice.

[ANOTHER PLACE] [A FEW]

I was broken into a couple times years later, in my single apartment. One time I'd had everything on the floor, of course, my 4 track recorder, typewriter and my purse. I was sleeping on the couch, the back of which was up against the windows, which opened out to a small alleyway between the apartment buildings. Whoever looked in the window couldn't see me asleep on the couch, and one night I woke up to a strange clicking sound. Right above me someone had shoved a curtain rod in the window, which was wavering above my head, ~~and~~ the end ~~had~~ been bent into a hook and ~~they were~~ fishing for my purse on the floor, dragging it toward the window. I leapt up and grabbed the rod and madly thrust it out the window, hopefully into the face of whoever was out there in the dark, screaming 'I'll blow your fucking head off, motherfucker!'

[margin notes: "what had been?", "all the while", "THIN (OLD)", "WAS RAKING THE CARPET"]

Same apartment. Recording. Playing bass with headphones on. I see the doorknob wiggle and the door shake and realize someone's trying to break in. Once again, 'I'll blow your head off, motherfucker!' This time I call the cops, ~~and they~~ don't come but spend some time on the phone with me. 'If you were my daughter' he says, 'I'd tell you to buy a gun'. He then tells me about a woman who called 911 when someone was breaking into her house, and over

[margin notes: "WHO", "A NICE CALM DESK SARGEANT"]

the phone you hear her ~~could~~ and then
screaming, ~~the guy~~ someone kick down the
door, a shot, and then
nothing..and then someone hangs
up the phone.

Some years later, I'm plagued by
a rather dedicated stalker. This
guy starts pissing in my car,
leaving little clues around, like a
cigarette pack on a windowsill. I
was living in Silver Lake then,
on a hillside with an empty lot
next to the house, really nice
with lots of trees, green. I loved
that house. On one of the worst
corners in L.A., but really
beautiful, really sweet. One day I
look out the kitchen door and
he's standing there, a blonde blue
eyed white guy, but with
a massive black mustache
painted under his nose with
magic marker or something and
a backwards baseball cap on his
head. 'Get the FUCK off my
property!' I'm screaming ~~at the~~ BUT
top of my lungs, he doesn't seem
fazed at all.
I mean, he's right there at my
door, and I'm ballistic. He finally

HER BEGGING + SCREAMING + then

= PHSYCHO =

← FURIOUS CHIHUAHUA

goes away, and I decide to put up an 8 foot fence..2 feet higher than was legal...wrought iron with death blades on top, screw this, I'm well pissed off now, and this
guy is obviously disturbed...I'd found the lot next door under a tree, a t-shirt and a huge PDF, which is a physicians' desk reference, a massive encyclopedia of pharmaceutical drugs. What the living hell is this guy about? I figured
he was some escaped mental patient, but it was getting weird. So the fence went up, and I bought a can of mace.

I'd been at the studio one day and came home that night and unlocked the gate at street level and took my guitars out of the car, placed them inside the gate, closed it behind me, picked them up and proceeded to climb the concrete stairs up to the front door of my house. I get almost all the way up and notice a shadowy figure on the porch, waiting. I lost my mind

completely, and dropped the guitars. 'What the fuck are you doing here?' I screamed, truly upset, really deranged by this point, because I don't know what this guy's about, what he wants, who he thinks I am, I'm just losing it. 'I need to keep an eye on you!' he says, now coming down the stairs toward me. 'I told you I was gonna fuck you up if you ever came on my property again! I told you!' and he's standing there babbling some shit about how he needs to watch me. I'm completely hysterical now but leave the guitars on the stairs,
go back down to my car, get the can of mace, come back up the stairs, and straight-arm the can of mace right at his face. 'You have to leave. I'm counting to ten and you have to be gone'. 10. 9. 8. 7.." he's babbling some kind of shit
and who cares what it was: '6.5.4.3.2...1." I prayed it would work and hit the button. The spray gushed out in a thick mist right in his face, and he held his

I WAS HYSTERICAL. YOU CAN'T IMAGINE.

hands up, and went down like a
fuckin' bug, crumpled down on
the stairs,
screaming:

'you had NO probable cause!"

Now that was the last thing I
expected to hear. By this time,
the Guatamalan family who
rented the front house had come
out and had called 911, and in a
few minutes a black and white
showed up, a couple cops, one of
them
a blonde woman. The bastard
would not get up on his feet no
matter what they did, and they
had to call an ambulance. It had
turned into quite the scene, with
the fucker twitching around on
the stairs saying over and over,
'you had no probable cause'. I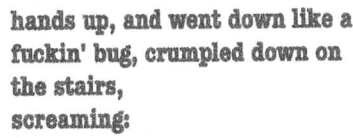
was furious, not to mention HAD
drained from having to deal with
this psycho for months, who, as it
turned out, had even been living
under the floors of women's
houses, watching them from
under their own floors. They
caught him because he'd built a

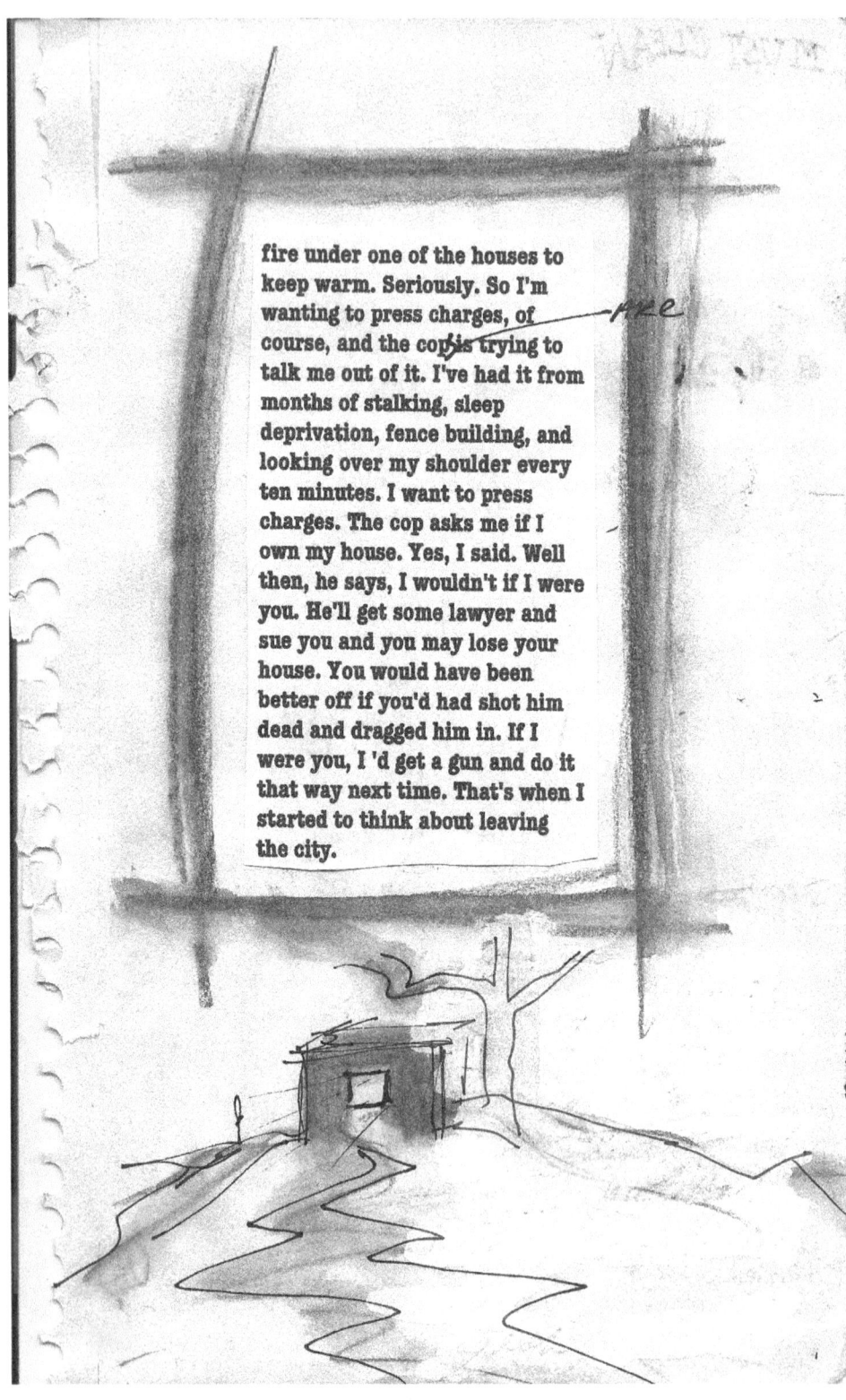

fire under one of the houses to keep warm. Seriously. So I'm wanting to press charges, of course, and the cop is trying to talk me out of it. I've had it from months of stalking, sleep deprivation, fence building, and looking over my shoulder every ten minutes. I want to press charges. The cop asks me if I own my house. Yes, I said. Well then, he says, I wouldn't if I were you. He'll get some lawyer and sue you and you may lose your house. You would have been better off if you'd had shot him dead and dragged him in. If I were you, I'd get a gun and do it that way next time. That's when I started to think about leaving the city.

When did I become this?
Uneven in my skin
Waves + water, bricks + stones
& music in between
in the empty spaces
Holding me together
Keep my cells from flying apart

I LIKE MY JAZZ ON VINYL
AND MY COFFEE BLACK
I FACE FORWARD
I DON'T LOOK BACK
I LIKE MY TEQUILA
STRAIGHT
& MY STORIES TRUE
YOU'RE THE REAL DEAL
BABY
AND I SURE LIKE YOU

form the perfect 2" foam head at the top of the pint, possibly more, depending on your choice of brew.

there's a huge tower on the corner of Sunset & Vine, there used to be a trendy bar at the top, that's been gone awhile ~~but~~ BUT even before that,..when there was still Wallach's Music City, the old music store on Vine, ~~was there,~~ near the Hollywood Palace. — WALLACH'S WAS RIGHT NEXT TO THE HOLLYWOOD PALACE, NOW "THE AVALON" I THINK.

THE BOSS — Anyway, I was young, and had answered an ad for a job in that building. I doubt I can use his real name but ~~he~~ was a black guy who ran some hustle charging people to listen to their demos and then "produce" their demos, "shop" them, whatever. He wasn't there ~~much~~ ONLY, and it was ~~me~~ MOST OF THE TIME

THE BOSS — and another girl. ~~I was really into it,~~ I'm made of the stuff that takes on everything I do pretty seriously, even at that age. ~~He~~ reminded me of Mr. Jefferson on the Jeffersons, all seventies 'fro and platforms. Tourists would stumble in off the bus, bring their music or just even sit and play for me,

& my job was to listen and sell them a 'recording package' for the 'producers' to take over and demo. I loved it and really got into it, and had that mentality anyway that everybody who came in deserved a song to be treated well ~~to the best~~ AND HAD

YOUR SELF — potential, etc. I was psyched to have my first job in Hollywood in the music business, and of course sincerely loved music and understood what it was like to walk into an office and put it on the line just off the bus, living in your car, whatever...

John

I'd pop a cassette (THIER) into the machine, listen, and truly heard a lot of heart in a lot of those little demos from ~~these~~ some fresh-faced kids, ~~and I think the recording package... which they had to 'qualify' for,~~ WITH THIER ANXIOUS PARENTS BESIDE THEM ~~although~~ I know now that my mostly-absentee boss couldn't have cared less about ~~the~~ music, ~~was~~ about $800.00, all in, I worked like crazy, and was so excited, stomping off to work from my Aunt's place off Sunset in my platforms, all dedicated, determined, LIKE A Good little worker bee.

PER "SUCKER".

Across Sunset, on Vine, ~~was~~ at Wallach's Music City, ~~and~~ I'd put on layaway a new guitar.. an Ovation. I couldn't wait to get that guitar out. Every day I was closer to making the final $20 payment and I would be able to take that guitar home.

THE day I got the new job.

I worked and walked and did my thing and I was psyched. I'd sold well, and the most important thing was I took these people's music every bit as seriously as they did. JB did not.

TO ME

He was never there - people would call for him all day, and he was never there - but I was the eager, Girl Scout receptionist, and did a good job. I took messages, but they were startin' to get hostile...! bill collectors, angry clients waiting for their "SESSIONS" to be booked.

I was also counting on my first paycheck to cross the street to Wallachs to get my guitar. Timelines blur but my only little nylon string *acoustic guitar* had been stolen straight out of my little house in the middle of

the day in North Hollywood, and I was devastated. I hadn't been without a guitar since I was 9.

The Mon payday, JB came in *across from my desk* and sat and said: 'I just don't have the money to pay you'. Eyes as cold as a snake. It

was obviously a front for something *else entirely,* and I was maybe doing too good of a job.

I was punched in the stomach and the only thing I could think of was how the fuck am I ever going to get my guitar? Never mind rent, never mind anything...but I had to have a guitar.

A client ~~Someone~~ had given me money orders for a session that day...somebody who'*d* ~~been sold by me~~ *I'd sold a "session" to,* who I'd talked out of their money. ~~And~~ I never lied to anyone, I'*d* *until now* believed ~~the~~ company line, I'*d* really believed this was a legit thing.

As he sat there across ~~from~~ *WHY* me, telling me ~~he~~ couldn't pay me for the last 2 weeks, I knew in my head exactly what I was going to do. **AFTER HE LEFT,** I took those money orders and I forged his name. My cousin, who was staying with me at my Aunt's in Hollywood off Las Palmas & Franklin, remembers: 'you said, 'come on, we're going to buy a guitar'! and I went to Wallach's and I got my Ovation, and never went back to that building.

Of course, the dude called me and asked about the missing money orders, but I knew by then he was a criminal and a hustler, and he knew I knew ~~he was, as well,~~ *THAT, TOO,* and he owed me straight up and he knew it, and it was easy, and he was stupid, and underestimated my desperation.

So ~~and~~ I had my guitar, which was all I needed and maybe he learned to not fuck with a little scrappy broke-ass determined Hollywood street rat ever *AGAIN*.

Or to fuck with people's dreams.

I've been a Baja rat since I was young, Baja California being the lower half of the state, which is Mexico. At one time the Jesuits thought that bit of land was an island. There are unmarked caves and ancient rock paintings and before I got a place down near La Bufadora, the blowhole, I used to cruise down with Cheech and stay at a place called La Fonda. La Fonda has been there forever, an old hotel with dry palapas shading rickety wooden porches on the cliff and long stone steps down to the beach. The place has a great bar and a Sunday brunch that brings people in taxis from across the border. I'd take a stack of books and my cassette recorder and a guitar and head down for a couple days. La Fonda had no phones or bell desk or anything back then. I remember rolling in one night in the wee hours, it must have been 3:00 a.m., and we were starving.

One of the janitors let us in a room and for $20 he cooked us up an amazing plate of fish, rice and beans with a couple of shots of tequila alongside. The owner of the place, Dimitri, who has since sold the place, I believe, is a Russian-American who looks exactly like the comedian Jonathan Winters. I loved staying at La Fonda because once you were there you didn't need to go anywhere else. The beach, the food, the bar, it was all there.

On one visit to La Fonda Cheech and I checked in and I plopped my backpack down on the bed and was ready to draw a nice bath when there was a knock at the door. A healthy looking young college jock apologized and said, "I left something here". I let him in, and he reached up to the canopy covering the bed to retrieve a plastic bag of weed.

Lance or Biff or whatever his name was left and I had a nice bath and Cheech, always hyper-aware, sensed my relaxation and curled up like a little round bagel on the pillow on the bed. I read a bit and had a nap.

I could hear the band start playing down in the bar below and the sun was setting over the ocean. I've been a lot of places in the world and on this planet I do not believe there is a more beautiful stretch of coastline than between Tijuana and Ensenada. Gorgeous, huge red cliffs and pure blue, deep water; dolphins and whales dancing along parallel to the beach. I've driven that coast too many times to count.

It's about time to head downstairs for a basket of tortilla chips and a few beers to bring back up to the room. I leave Cheech and step out to head down to the bar.

Halfway down the stairs I notice a pair of legs in gym shoes and white pants sticking out from under a bush on the hillside. This isn't particularly odd to me, as it's a weekend and the college kids are out in great, loud, stupid numbers and I don't think much about it. However, if the legs are still there when I come back up, I will have to address the situation.

When I come back up with my basket of thick, greasy slabs of tortilla and a couple of fat little brown bottles of Mexican beer the legs are still there, splayed out in bright white pants. No way to ignore this now, I lean down and ask,

"Are you ok? Hello?"

The legs started to move, and I heard someone crying.

She crawled out from under the bush, young and blonde, mascara-streaked. "Thank you! Thank you! People have been walking by me all night and nobody even stopped! Thank you!"

And I was one of them, I thought. She needed to use the bathroom, so I took her upstairs.

She pissed and felt better. She was hysterical. I hugged her and the crucifix I wore around my neck kept tangling up in the lace of her blouse over her left breast. She was teary and sad and apparently had come down from San Diego on her boyfriend's yacht and they'd fought and he had left her there at the bar, She didn't know shit about Mexico or where she was and it was her birthday and

she was just a mess.

I cracked a beer for her and she started to talk. She'd been a 'novice', that is, a young nun at some convent around San Diego. Her boyfriend, the one that had left her that night on her birthday in the bushes outside my room had been the gardener at the convent or nunnery or wherever the hell nuns live. She'd fallen hard for him and had left the Order.

Cheech, still curled up on the pillow next to me on the bed, opens one eye, warily.

The Nun had fallen in love with the gardener and had left the Order, after much prayer, tears, gnashing of teeth, etc. Apparently this is the guy who dumped her tonight, on her birthday. The young novice was rewarded 4 HER HAVING for falling GIN in love with a mere mortal with breast cancer, and in fact, where my crucifix had been getting caught in the lace of her blouse over her left breast was not a left breast at all, but a prosthetic.

The surgeon that had removed her left breast had been her own father, insisting he perform the surgery himself. Luckily he was indeed a surgeon.

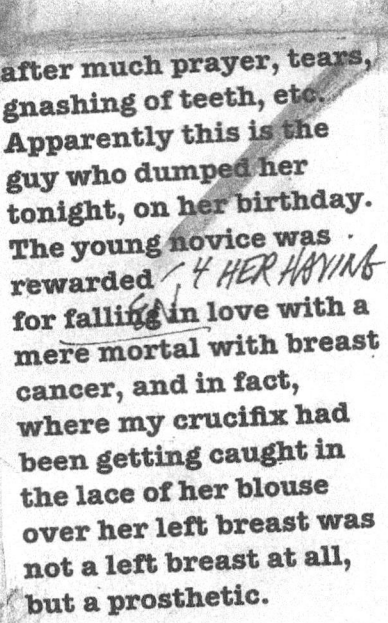

Sometimes in life shit gets so weird all you can do is ride the wave to the beach, as it were, and I watched her talk and I'm

realizing I found a titless nun in the bushes on the way down to the bar and someone elses' half-pound of weed in my bed and I've only been here a couple hours and she's telling me this story and wiping her nose and crying and then all of a sudden, as if she'd just woken up, looks around the room
and weirdly at me and says, "what are you doing here? Are you by yourself?"

Cheech, a little brown muffin on the pillow on the bed again opens one eye in my direction. God rest her little Chihuahua soul, she lived 20 years of my life with me.

The Nun looked scared,

like I was some crazy lesbian serial killer, and straightened herself up. "I should go".

"Are you sure?" I said. "I could give you a ride to the border?"

"No" she said. "He'll be back. I"d better go down." and she clutched a cellophane-wrapped bad tourist little souvenir scene made of seashells, and I can't remember where it came from.

"Ok." and then she took her gold bracelet off her arm and gave it to me. "Take this!"

"Really?" I said, and took the twisted gold. A gift of

gold from a one-breasted nun I found in the bushes in Mexico.

Her name was Mary. She'd scribbled her number and I think I called her once and left a message, but what was there to say, really, after that?

I still have the gold bracelet.

and dead seah or $155

having a drink with Frida

*... what will you say of me,
you, who never knew my heart?*

X 62   MUSIC 1st

I do notice lyrical trends, though: single words; when rhythms changed in the '80's I noticed lyrics change also.

The tone + timbre + color of the music should compliment the lyrics — or vice versa, whichever come first —

So a single word title, or name; can be as touching and personal as an entire poem, or lyric —

especially when married to sound.

can give the word a whole new meaning

whichever comes 1st or last

GHOST OF A TEXAS LADIES MAN
(Walking In London, Concrete Blonde)

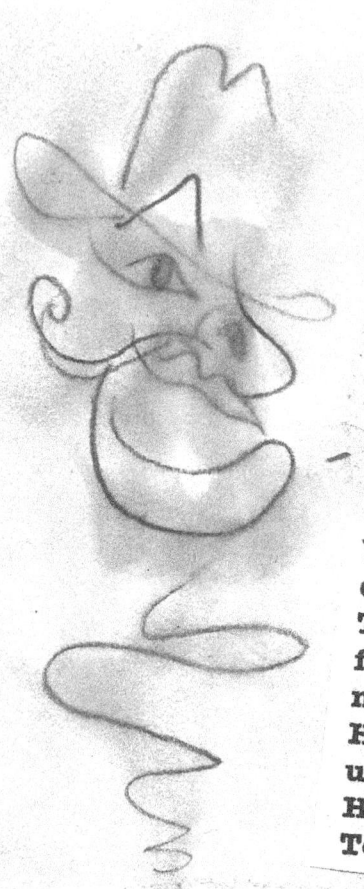

I saw a face in the shower door
A cowboy smile
Came and faded
I reached for my towel on the floor
I didn't think it was exactly where I'd laid it

You don't scare me, you don't scare me, I said
To whatever it was floating in the air above my bed
He knew I'd understand
He was the Ghost of a Texas Ladies' Man.

I reached to turn out the light
He wouldn't let me get near it
He seemed so glad to see a woman in the flesh,
And I really liked his spirit

You don't scare me you don't scare me I cried
To my ectoplasmic lover from the other side
He knew I'd understand
He was the Ghost of a Texas Ladie's Man

We were on the road opening for Sting one summer, and had a bus. Bus drivers like to drive at night because there's less traffic, etc., and we would generally pull into a hotel in the morning with everybody still asleep on the bus. I was traveling with my cat, Bear, on that tour, and we pulled into the Driskill Hotel in Austin pretty early in the morning. I had my luggage and Bear's travel-kennel thing, so I would need to make two trips from the bus up to my room. I checked in and noticed the massive portrait of Colonel Driskill behind the desk. I love old hotels and was struck by it right away. I hauled Bear in his kennel up to my room on the 5th floor, left him and headed back down to the bus for the rest of my luggage, but when I came back up to my room the key wouldn't open the lock. It wasn't one of those credit-card

plastic keys, either, it was a proper heavy big brass one. Weird. I went down to the desk.

"My key won't work'. I said.

The guys behind the next glanced at each other nervously.

"Would you like breakfast?" one of them said, motioning toward the dining room off the lobby. "Please have breakfast on the hotel until we can send an engineer up to let you in your room."

Engineer? Free breakfast? Ok, I thought, so I took him up on it and after a quick breakfast we went up to the 5th floor.

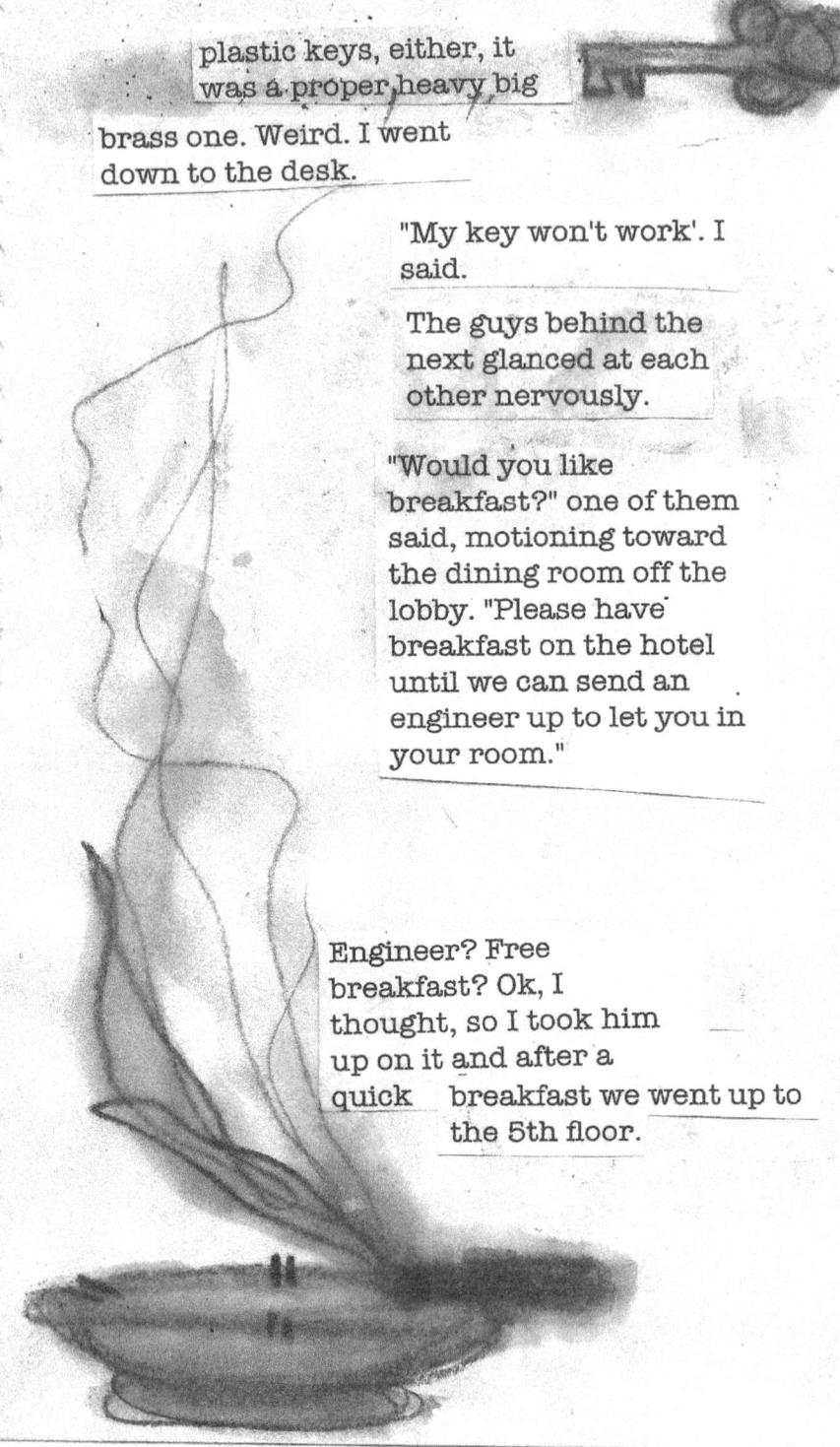

The 'engineer' was nervous and fidgety, and stuck the key from his master keyring into the lock and turned it. It opened easily.

JANITOR (SCARED)

It was an off-kilter sort of day, the TV would work, then it wouldn't, I kept dropping things, things were falling off the bed, the desk.

It was a late night, being in Austin, and after the gig we hung out with some friends afterward and I got back to the hotel around 3:00 a.m.

When I got up to my room, Bear was odd. Cats, at night, should be bouncing off walls, playing hockey in the bathroom with bottlecaps, slapping your head in the dark. Bear was huddled on the pillow in the middle of the bed.

I started undressing and headed into the bathroom to shower when I had a strong feeling someone was watching me. I walked around the suite and drew the curtains, although I was on the 5th floor and there was no one to see in the window. Still, I felt creepy, like someone was there. I took a bath and headed to bed. On the nightstand beside the bed was a small lamp with a pullchain, the old kind, with

a silk shade.

I pulled the chain, the light went out, and I turned over to sleep. The light came back on. I turned, reached over and pulled the chain. The light went out. I turned over. The light came back on.

It was starting to dawn on me there was something up here. I'd been feeling creepy all day, and now I was sure someone was messing with me. I turned over and pulled the chain again, and waited in the dark.

For not even a minute. The light came on again. I need a lot of sleep on the road and it was almost 4:00 a.m. I reached over and pulled the cord out of the socket in the wall.

"I know you're here." I said out loud in the dark. "I know you're here and you won't hurt me, but I have to get to sleep, it's late and I'm tired."

Very slowly, as if a hand were pushing it from the other side, the heavy closet door opened, and the closet light, which had been left on, shone out into a single beam onto the rug. As the door opened wider and wider, the beam of light from the closet grew wider and wider and longer and finally shone right on me, by this time, sitting straight up in complete disbelief, naked in bed.

Naked! In bed! The ghost wanted to see me naked!

That was it, he was watching me take a bath, he wanted to see me and wanted the lights left on!

Since then I've learned that the Driskill is famously haunted by a ghost that likes to have his way with the ladies, especially on the 5th floor, although he's been seen playing the piano in the mezzanine, these days kept locked closed.

His ghostly activities have included slapping a drink out of a woman's hand in the bar, grabbing a female guests' ankle while she slept before disappearing under the bed. The woman called the desk hysterically, and a pair of nervous hotel security guards came up to her room, guns drawn, but wouldn't look under the bed.

also the housekeepers know all about him?

Whenever I'm in Austin I drink at the Driskill bar. The veteran bartenders don't put much stock in the ghost stories, but I'm a believer for sure.

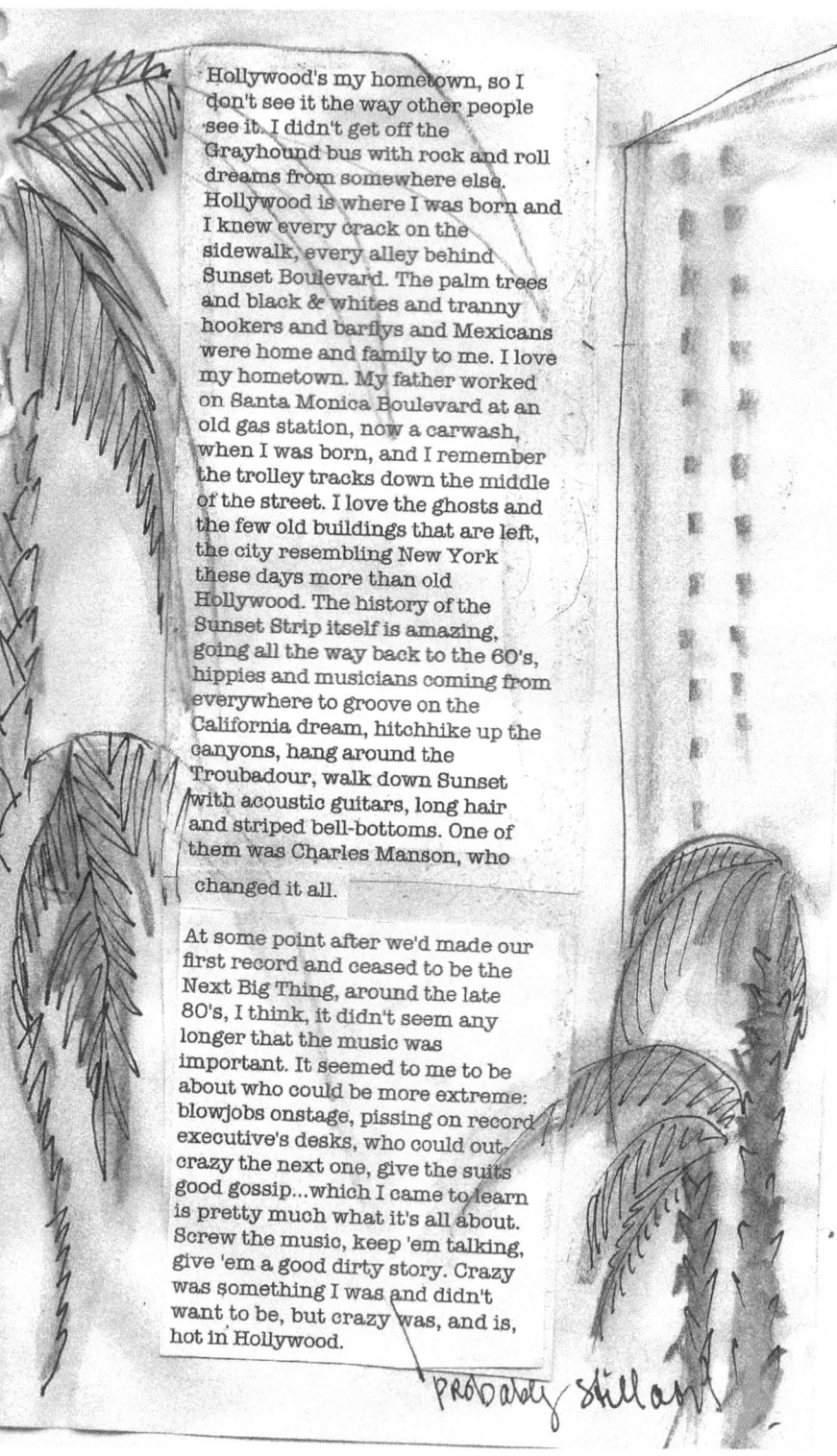

Hollywood's my hometown, so I don't see it the way other people see it. I didn't get off the Grayhound bus with rock and roll dreams from somewhere else. Hollywood is where I was born and I knew every crack on the sidewalk, every alley behind Sunset Boulevard. The palm trees and black & whites and tranny hookers and barflys and Mexicans were home and family to me. I love my hometown. My father worked on Santa Monica Boulevard at an old gas station, now a carwash, when I was born, and I remember the trolley tracks down the middle of the street. I love the ghosts and the few old buildings that are left, the city resembling New York these days more than old Hollywood. The history of the Sunset Strip itself is amazing, going all the way back to the 60's, hippies and musicians coming from everywhere to groove on the California dream, hitchhike up the canyons, hang around the Troubadour, walk down Sunset with acoustic guitars, long hair and striped bell-bottoms. One of them was Charles Manson, who changed it all.

At some point after we'd made our first record and ceased to be the Next Big Thing, around the late 80's, I think, it didn't seem any longer that the music was important. It seemed to me to be about who could be more extreme: blowjobs onstage, pissing on record executive's desks, who could out-crazy the next one, give the suits good gossip...which I came to learn is pretty much what it's all about. Screw the music, keep 'em talking, give 'em a good dirty story. Crazy was something I was and didn't want to be, but crazy was, and is, hot in Hollywood.

PROBably still am

Joey, baby.
~~Dont get crazy~~
Detours, fences
I get defensive
I know you've heard it all before
So I don't say it any more
I just stand by & let you
fight your secret war.
And though I used 2 wonder why
I used to cry till I was dry
Still sometimes I get a
strange pain inside.

at some point in the ~~somewhere~~ 90's. Marc Moreland and I were in a bar ~~in Europe somewhere~~, or London. Could have even been Mexico. We were knocking back shots and beers. Marc was, as usual, smoking.

We sat and drank, doughnuts of smoke circling our heads, an ashy veil of haze between us.

"Is "Joey" about me?" said Marc, hitting his cigarette.

"Yeah" I said, sipping my beer.

Marc thought for a minute, and blew a stream of smoke. ↓ long, slow

"Do you owe me money?" he said.

"No." I said.

"Oh. Okay." he said, and picked up his drink.

We sure had a good time, didn't we?

FIN

www.ingramcontent.com/pod-product-compliance
Lightning Source LLC
Chambersburg PA
CBHW060034180426
43196CB00045B/2670